Wesley E. Walker

SPOUSE'S

THERAPY

Discovere what

strengthens relationship

Develop a stronger bond in just a few weeks.

Every partnership occasionally faces difficulties. Regardless of how much you care for each other or how long you've been married, learning how to resolve disputes is a lifelong process. This book teaches you how to handle it more politely and successfully so that you may build a solid basis for communication and get even more enjoyment from one another.

What distinguishes this book from other romance novels

It offers ten detailed guidelines that will assist you in developing a healthier relationship and force your partner to grow to love you even more.

.

CHAPTER 1

Wesley Walker has chosen to provide some of their greatest advice on divorce prevention after years of compiling stories on the best and worst methods to handle marriage, separation, and divorce. These ten recommendations will either help you in your subsequent relationships or bring you to the point where you desire to straighten things out with your existing spouse. In either case, reading this advise is worthwhile.

Make time each day to communicate with your spouse in a caring manner.

Spending even just 15 minutes a day together solely can increase a couple's chances of having a successful marriage. You may get up a little earlier, for instance, and utilize the extra time in bed to cuddle, make love, and reiterating your commitment to one another. Spend time together each day talking about important things, listening intently like you did when you were dating, touching, cuddling, and otherwise expressing your affection for one another, sharing your feelings about your marriage, and discussing your aspirations for the union and your lives.

Being emotionally, physically, and sexually connected to your partner is crucial because it promotes your joint development as a married couple. Your marriage won't develop to its full potential if you and your husband or wife simply go about your daily business, leave each other alone, and never actually spend time interacting. Growing apart is one of the consequences of not communicating with your partner.You obviously love your spouse more than anything else, right? Show your spouse that you love them by making conscious efforts to connect with them on a daily basis. What is preventing you from connecting with your husband or wife every day? Have you attempted to contact them in any way?

Make it a point to communicate with your spouse every day!

Everyday ways to connect with your spouse

Kiss, hug, or cuddle your partner.

Exercise together, go for a run, jog, or visit the gym, for example.

Take a walk together and try walking while holding each other's hands.

Listen to your favorite music and dance.

Together, read a book.

It could be a religious book, a marriage book, a self-help book, fiction, etc.

Pray or meditate as a group.

Have a more in-depth discussion.

Talk about the highlights of your day, what you've been learning, what's been difficult, or anything else interesting that comes to mind! Oh, and pay close attention when your spouse is speaking. Use questions for couples to initiate deeper discussions. Remember that you are communicating with your spouse and that your full attention is required.

Prepare a meal and eat it as a family. This could easily be breakfast, lunch, or dinner.

Tell your spouse how much you adore and value them. Be grateful for their lives and thank them for making the decision to live.

choosing to spend every day of their lives with you

Watch TV shows and movies with your friends. It's Shark Tank for us.

Take a bath or shower together.

Have some sex. Take your time, too. As you experiment, explore, savor, and worship. Candles, music, and toys help to set the tone.

Do errands and chores together. For example, grocery shopping, dish washing, house cleaning, and so on.

Compliment your spouse sincerely.

Make a date night.

Eye-to-eye contact This can be accomplished through tantric breathing, sitting near them and conversing, or playing a game.

Make them smile, share a laugh, and dream together.

Flirt with one another.

Send your spouse a love/romantic/encouraging text message.

Surprise them with a small gesture. It could be a note, flowers, or something else., a small gift, doing their chores for them, making their favorite dessert, purchasing a book or latte for them The options are limitless!

Play enjoyable games with your friends. Check out this list of the best couples board, card, and dice games.

CHAPITRE 2

Every day, say something nice to your spouse. And take it seriously!

Compliment your spouse on a regular basis, both privately and in public. Even if your partner initially appears embarrassed or dismissive, the glow of genuine praise lasts a long time.

Compliments to Give to Your Spouse

Compliments are beneficial to your marriage because they make your spouse feel more confident and content, and a confident and contented spouse is a much more pleasant companion to be with. However, while compliments generally produce a desirable outcome, that should not be your motivation for using them. They should be genuine and heartfelt, not something you say just to get the desired effect.

You may believe that complimenting your spouse is a simple task. You make your partner happy by saying something nice, right? No, it does not. Compliments can be difficult to receive. It must be consistent with your spouse's core values in order to have a positive impact on his or her self-esteem. It will fall flat if your spouse does not see the value in what you are complimenting him or her on. Something you may consider a genuine compliment may appear lame or even insulting to your spouse. That being said, if you appreciate your spouse and are unsure what to say to properly express your appreciation, here are some universally good compliments.

"You're very thoughtful."

A little gratitude goes a long way in marriages, and it can even lead to a lower divorce rate. So, if your spouse does something nice for you without being asked, don't ignore it. Recognize the thoughtfulness he or she has shown you, even if it is small. It's easy to overlook the many helpful little things your spouse does on a daily basis. Only the extravagant attract attention. Consider all of the wonderful, non-glamorous things your spouse does for you on a daily basis. It could be as simple as making you a cup of coffee, doing your laundry, filling up your car with gas so you don't have to, or cooking dinner.The list goes on and on. Tell your spouse how much you value these things.

"You work extremely hard."

You and your spouse both put in a lot of effort. Most likely, you both work outside the home for the majority of the day and then return home to tend to your respective household duties. This happens on a daily basis. It can be exhausting to build a life together. The daily grind wears everyone down, including your spouse, so show your spouse that you appreciate how hard he or

She works for the sake of your family.

"You do so much for me, and I am very grateful."

When you're married, you help each other without expecting anything in return. Love, not accolades, motivates you to serve one another. However, there are two words in the English language that are extremely powerful and that every human being craves to hear: "Thank you." Try saying, "You do so much for me, and I am very thankful for you," the next time your spouse does something to lighten your load, such as cooking dinner or doing the laundry.Recognize that they did what you asked them to do and that you appreciate their cooperation. According to research, when you express gratitude to someone for an act of service, the person you thanked is more likely to want to help you again in the future. Everyone wants to feel needed by someone. When you express gratitude to your spouse, you are expressing your need for him or her and fulfilling a deep human desire within your partner.

"You look fantastic."

There are many people who are self-conscious about their bodies in today's world. When Hollywood and social media only show the perfect, edited versions of people, it's difficult for both men and women to feel good about themselves.Body image can influence how well a person performs in a variety of situations. A negative body image can have an impact on your partner's job confidence, relationship satisfaction, and even their mental health. It's easy to criticize your spouse when they dress or do their hair in a way you don't like. This can make your spouse depressed and make them feel bad about themselves. Instead, try to always compliment them when you think they are particularly attractive. Your spouse is likely to want to dress and do their hair like that again and again because of the positive attention you are giving them.They want to look good for you, and in this case, positive reinforcement works better than criticism.

"I admire you."Respect is the bedrock of any marriage. Respect is the foundation of everything that constitutes a great marriage. What factors contribute to a successful marriage? Loyalty, faithfulness, thoughtfulness, patience, consideration, empathy, and compassion are all virtues. Yes, all of these qualities are required, but they do not appear out of nowhere. They are all based on mutual respect.

"I respect you" is probably not a commonly used phrase. This is most likely due to the fact that it is frequently demonstrated through actions. If someone truly respects you, you will notice how they treat you, not necessarily how they treat others.While actions definitely speak louder than words in this case, misunderstandings do occur from time to time, and your partner may misinterpret something you do. It could have been a movement, a facial expression, or the tone of your voice. Perhaps you recently had a heated argument. Whatever it was, you inadvertently made your spouse feel disrespected. This is why it is important to show and vocalize your respect for your spouse.

"You Make An Excellent Wife."

Your partner needs to hear how much you appreciate them as a husband or wife. "You are a great spouse," may appear cheesy on the surface because it is such a simple statement, but it speaks volumes.It will sound like music to your spouse. Why? Because that is what your spouse strives for every day. Sure, they will make mistakes because no one is perfect. But, in the end, your spouse wants to be the best.

Every now and then, your spouse requires affirmation. They need a reminder that even if things aren't perfect, you still love them and consider yourself lucky to be married to them. You still think they're a fantastic spouse. The more you tell them, the more your spouse will think of you as a wonderful spouse. Positive affirmations should be reinforced in your spouse's mind because people often become what they believe they are. Do you want a wonderful spouse? Assist them in thinking like one.

Positive Remarks for Your Spouse

Try one of the above compliments on your spouse the next time you want to make them feel loved and valued. Your marriage will probably be considerably happier as a result of how much they will value your compassion. Couples therapy can be a helpful resource if, for whatever reason, your partner still doesn't feel valued in your marriage. Your spouse's feelings will be addressed, and a counselor will assist you in using productive communication techniques. Giving compliments should always be a top priority in your marriage since you and your spouse need to feel valued by one another.

CHAPTER 3

Love your mate in the manner he/she needs to be adored.

We frequently wrongly expect that the things that touch our hearts the most profoundly will influence our accomplice similarly. For example, you might think red roses are the ideal gift, however to your companion, they address a misuse of cash and a sensitivity assault. On the off chance that you don't as of now have the foggiest idea, figure out what your life partner longs for, and afterward convey it with affection — and no remarks about the fact that it is to need a cordless drill/an excursion on the family room floor/a fish goulash. Keep in mind: the best gift is something your mate needs — not only something you need him/her to have.

Pay attention to what your mate is talking about.

At the point when we invest a ton of energy with somebody, from one viewpoint we might feel we know them good than any other individual. Then again, we might quit seeing specific things about them as they become more recognizable to us. This isn't on the grounds that we're not intrigued or couldn't care less. It's frequently in light of the fact that our lives can get going, routinized, or agreeable so that we stop effectively getting to know the other individual.

Focusing on what our accomplice says seems like the clearest guidance we'll at any point hear, however it's something we need to remind ourselves to continue to do. Give careful consideration of when they notice something that is important to them or something that invigorates them. Urge them to be vocal about and request what they need.

Focus on how they express their sentiments.

As well as hearing what they express, we ought to continuously attempt to see what illuminates our accomplice. It's quite simple to recognize the times where they appear to be exhausted and continue to actually take a look at their telephones from those where they're grinning and energized. This doesn't mean we're answerable for fulfilling them 100% of the time. It's simply an approach to being adjusted and delicate to what causes them wake up and to feel most themselves. This mindfulness assists us with genuinely knowing our accomplice and comprehend the sorts of things that cause them to feel seen and cherished.

Check in with your accomplice (and yourself).

Not even one of us are telepaths, and we can't be anticipated to intuit what someone else needs and needs consistently. It's more than OK to seek clarification on some pressing issues and urge our accomplice to tell us where they're at and what they need from us. By that equivalent measure, we ought to continue to check in with ourselves about what we want and need to cause us to feel cherished and satisfied. However much as could reasonably be expected, we ought to open up to our accomplice about these things - not anticipating that they should mind read by the same token. By empowering a free and regular this way and that, we become more helpless against one another and more equipped for offering each other what we truly care about.

Notice how they express love.

Chances are, the warm ways our accomplice treats us are to some degree intelligent of a way they appreciate being dealt with. On the off chance that they search out a ton of actual contact or enjoy little demonstrations of liberality and benevolence, they might partake in something very similar from us. Obviously, this doesn't need to be taken in a real sense, and no undertaking should be matched precisely. For instance, it's entirely normal for every individual to carry specific interesting things to the relationship. One accomplice might just appreciate doing the other's clothing, since it fulfills them, while the other favors large, clearing heartfelt motions. The point here isn't to say that we shouldn't have our own singular approaches to being wanting to one another. Rather, it's simply one more way we can be careful and sensitive to specific activities that could cause our accomplice to feel recognized.

Acknowledge your accomplice's necessities as not the same as your own.

Connections ought not be about penance. On the off chance that satisfying someone else on a predictable premise implies making ourselves hopeless, something may truly be off and the relationship might worth inspect. In any case, we ought to continuously be embracing of the way that our accomplice is a different individual from ourselves. While making each other cheerful can be our very own tremendous piece satisfaction, every one of our sentiments exist separate from the other's.

This is all to say that it's acceptable for you to need more love and for your accomplice to need more correspondence. It's acceptable for one individual to feel more cherished by their accomplice cleaning the counter than saying "I love you." Others could require the words. We each have various things to offer that would be useful and propose to one another. It's excessive for every one of our longings to match up precisely consistently to partake in an equivalent and adoring relationship. The only thing that is important is that every one of us keeps an open progression of interest, inventiveness, and energy around communicating our affection to somebody we helpfully as of now love. Couples who persistently analyze and characterize how love affects every one of them have the most obvious opportunity with regards to keeping that feeling invigorated, both in their accomplice and in themselves.

CHAPTER 4

Deal with your appearance.

Put your best self forward for your life partner. Lose the junky sweat pants or frayed sweater he/she detests so a lot; you can find other agreeable garments that are certainly not a total mood killer for your accomplice. This likewise implies dealing with your wellbeing — including eating appropriately and practicing routinely.

Wonder why you need to work on your appearance. Is it safe to say that you are doing this for yourself or another person? What do you expect to accomplish by working on your appearance?

Assuming that you're attempting to change how you look with the expectations of drawing in somebody, be cautious that you stay consistent with yourself as you go through the accompanying advances. Just make the wisest decision for you.

Recognize what you like and what you could do without about your appearance. A large portion of us find it more straightforward to distinguish what we could do without about ourselves, yet it's essential to recognize a few beneficial things, as well.

When you sort out what you like best about yourself, contemplate how you can play it up.

Be reasonable about what you can and can't change. You could find it valuable to make a rundown of what you like and could do without, and afterward reasonably consider what you can really change about yourself.

For instance, you can't change that you're short, however assuming you need to, you can give the deception of looking taller by wearing high heels (ladies) or shoes with thicker heels (men or ladies). There are additionally things you can do with your attire and hair to assist with giving the presence of length (for instance, assuming you're short, you should abstain from having extremely lengthy hair or wearing long coats that arrive at beneath the knees, as these things can make you look more limited).

Figure out how to adore your peculiarities. Perhaps you disdain a large portion of what you look like, yet your appearance isn't just about how generally alluring you are. As you work through the accompanying advances, attempt to move somewhere around one thing from your "could do without" rundown to your "like" list.

Perhaps you disdain that your hair is so thick, yet with the right hair style, items, and styling, you could possibly turn that around and truly love how you can manage your hair.

Be consistent with yourself. Preferably, further developing your appearance is tied in with letting your actual self radiate through. There's really no need to focus on fitting a standard ideal of what engaging quality is to society overall. As you work on working on your appearance, remember this.

Perhaps you feel most such as yourself with your normal hair and complexions, wearing unbiased apparel. Perhaps you feel most such as yourself with brightly colored hair, piercings, and hand-made, unique outfits. Try not to allow society to direct what the most ideal form of you resembles. You are the master on you.

Be delicate with yourself. For a few of us, resting easier thinking about our appearance may be basically as straightforward as getting another hair style; for other people, it very well may be a significantly longer, more troublesome interaction. Realize that we have all battled with fearlessness and keeping up with sound propensities. The key is to remain positive and, in particular, be thoughtful to yourself.

Assuming that you conclude that piece of your arrangement to further develop your appearance is to practice on a more regular basis, being delicate means being reasonable about what you can do — for instance, in the event that you don't work-out consistently, begin with two days every week and move up from that point. Being delicate likewise implies that when you miss a day or commit an error, you don't blow up at yourself; you simply recognize it, excuse yourself, and earnestly promise to begin new tomorrow.

Make a sensible activity plan. Having an unmistakable feeling of your objectives will assist you with remaining on track and on target. While making your activity arrangement, be mindful so as not to define an excessive number of objectives for yourself at one time. Assuming you roll out an excessive number of improvements on the double, you'll gamble with becoming overpowered and not having the option to stay aware of any of them.

If you conclude you need to get thinner, work on your skin, and rest better, you'll probably have to execute these progressions to your way of life in stages.

For instance, you could begin by practicing two times every week and focusing on cleaning up two times every day with a suitable cleaning agent (for example one for your skin type — dry, typical, mix, skin inflammation inclined) for the first or fourteen days.

Get it on paper. As you consider your intentions and plans for working on your appearance, monitor your contemplations and sentiments in a diary. Give a diary to working on your appearance. Compose your activity plan down in the diary with the goal that you can allude back to it.

Keep on keeping your diary as you foster new propensities for working on your appearance. This will assist you with assessing what works and what doesn't.

Be sensible and patient. Except if you have limitless assets and will go through a medical procedure, your outcomes will not be prompt. To work on your appearance in the long haul requires long haul way of life changes. Give yourself the reality you really want. Realize that this will be different for everybody relying upon their singular objectives and circumstances.

CHAPTER 5

Stay devoted.

The reasons you fall head over heels for somebody might be a secret, however the reasons we stay in affection are undeniably less confusing. A serious relationship implies you are bound to one another by an imperceptible yet substantial association. It is a guarantee frankly, faithful and to never deceive the other individual. The ideal accomplice treats you with generosity and warmth. You can depend on them, since they don't change on you. They are generally your ally. Dependability is the main part of a serious relationship. The following are a couple of motivations behind why it means a lot to search for a dependable accomplice.

Devoted is the Top Quality to Search for in an Accomplice. Dependability prompts areas of strength for a

On the off chance that you are steadfast seeing someone, will constantly show your accomplice your commitment to them. Thusly, you will make a profound close to home association. Reliability is the establishment and bedrock in any great relationship.

Trust guarantees a certain coexistence

At the point when you realize that your accomplice tells the truth and on your side, you can without hesitation face coexistence. You'll have a solid sense of security putting resources into different pieces of your life, since you have a steady relationship.

Assuming then again, your mate is faithless and deceitful, you are bound to hush up about things. It's difficult to confront life all alone! You shouldn't need to feel that you need to carry extra to the relationship, since they aren't completely dedicated.

Correspondence assembles trust among you and your accomplice

How would you make trust when you keep on misleading individuals nearest to you? Trustworthiness is one of the vital parts of a solid relationship. It assists us with staying away from destructive breaks of trust and sets practical assumptions. The ideal accomplice endeavors to carry on with an existence of uprightness, so there are no errors in their relationship.

Faithfulness opens you to shape a genuine association

Devotion is the best way to shape a genuine association. On the off chance that you are being unfaithful seeing someone, are controlling piece of yourself and will not have the option to shape areas of strength for a genuine association with your accomplice. You could have noteworthy minutes or transitory sentiments, in any case, it will self-destruct with the absence of trust.

Culpability will eat you from the back to front

Culpability is something entertaining. Until you experience it, you have no clue about what a hold it has over you. Untrustworthiness separates the great and damages your accomplice. The culpability you feel will likewise hurt you, and it will be challenging to live with yourself.

Being steadfast provides you with a deep satisfaction, particularly assuming that you realize that you treat your cooperate with graciousness, regard and genuineness. Being reliable seeing someone understanding that to be with somebody, you must accompany them 100%.

CHAPTER 6

Do things together.

One more typical element of long haul cheerful relationships is that the life partners consistently do things together that they view as tomfoolery and invigorating. Whether that is couples dancing, bowling, playing a game of cards, or skiing, partake in no less than one movement that you both partake in each week. Assuming that you have children, ensure to some extent half of these exercises are for yourself as well as your mate as it were.

Go Out on the town

The run of the mill supper and-a-film night out on the town is consistently perfect, yet some of the time you likewise need an unconstrained break from your daily practice. Break new ground: early lunch, karaoke, or a languid day at the recreation area consider dates, as well. Date evenings don't need to be costly to be fun, all things considered.

What should be done out on the town

a stroll in nature, Visit a historical center, Go deal hunting, Join a random data group, Go to a break room,

Visit the zoo, Go to an arcade or carnival, Attempt another eatery, Make another recipe together, Have a spa night at home, Take a dance class, Make a specialty together, Hit up a show or satire show, Take another exercise class together, Go to an open house, Visit a brewery or go to a wine sampling, Attempt roller skating, Host a party.

Travel

Gather your bag and move away for the evening, an end of the week, or seven days. A heartfelt escape re-energizes you both and gives you some quality time together away from your ordinary daily practice.

In the event that your financial plan is tight, select a one-night trip that is near and dear, and think about booking a home.

Eat Outside of what might be expected

Exhausted of your nearby cafés? Plan an outing to investigate an acclaimed café you never attempted. Pick a city that is not frightfully distant from home or go overboard and remain one night at a close by inn. Feasting off in an unexpected direction can give a heartfelt and new experience for both of you.

Investigate the Closest State Park

Investing energy outside accompanies a universe of advantages, including holding and making deep rooted recollections. Pack a knapsack and make a beeline for the closest state park for the afternoon. Get those endorphins rolling and go for a long climb together. Or on the other hand, set up for business for the evening and untruth next to each other looking at the stars.

Going out traveling together doesn't need to include a major financial plan or a long excursion to an extraordinary area. Visiting off in an unexpected direction spots in your own town or close by sights can likewise be an extraordinary method for partaking in the advantages of voyaging and investigating together.

Get Dynamic Together

Participating in proactive tasks together can likewise be an extraordinary method for getting to know each other. Luckily, there are a lot of good thoughts that will assist you with interfacing.

Work out

The advantages of practicing together are bounty. Not exclusively will you get to get to know one another, yet you'll likewise work on your general wellbeing, get in better shape, and even improve your sexual coexistence. Practice has been connected to further developed self-perception, decreased sexual and erectile brokenness, and short-and long haul excitement in ladies.

This could mean going for a stroll together, going to a yoga class, utilizing an activity application at home, or playing a wellness game on a computer game control center. Practicing together can likewise be as a demanding movement like composition a room, clearing out a cellar, or establishing a nursery.

Dance

Play those old records (assuming that you actually have them) or put on your number one playlist. Ask your accomplice for a dance in the kitchen. Or on the other hand, take your moves making the rounds and hit a dance club.

Investigate a Side interest Together

One more method for interfacing as a team is to hang out investigating a side interest. This can be something that you both appreciate doing, or you could appreciate helping each other investigate your singular advantages.

Begin Another Side interest

Settle on some shared interest and search for leisure activities you would partake in together. In the event that you can't settle on a movement you both appreciate, decide to do isolate leisure activities in a similar room or on a similar love seat. For example, assuming one individual likes to scrapbook, they can do that while their accomplice plays computer games.

Cook Together

Consider breaking out the estimating cups and cookbooks to flavor things up in the kitchen. In the event that you have youngsters, require no less than one night a month to have supper after the children head to sleep. Cook together and partake in a pleasant calm feast for only you two.

On the off chance that you can escape the house, taking a cooking class together is a great method for learning a few new recipes and cooking strategies.

Rearrange

Pick a space to rearrange together. It very well may be a room that needs a hierarchical makeover or one that you need to clean up since you use it frequently.

Brightening isn't tied in with being an expert inside originator. It's about the time you and your accomplice spend together while redesigning, reusing, or rethinking the necessities you have for a specific room or space in your home.

Attempting another side interest or action together can be a great method for holding. It tends to be an incredible method for accomplishing something you love with the individual you love.

Unwind Together

Getting dynamic and investigating side interests can be fun, yet in some cases you should accomplish something really unwinding or serene together. This can be an extraordinary chance to destress and loosen up while appreciating each other's conversation.

Share a Book

Twist up on the love seat or in bed and read a book together. Recite without holding back or read together discreetly. Begin your own confidential book club for you two. Talk about the books you're perusing espresso or your #1 dinner.

Pay attention to a Webcast or Book recording

Cuddle on the lounge chair and tune into a digital broadcast or book recording together. Pick something entertaining to add a little state of mind supporting giggling to your life, or something inspirational that can reinforce you as people and as a couple.

Mess around

Whether you're raising a ruckus around town together or plunking down with a decent game, tabletop game, or puzzle, games can be an incredible pressure reliever. Messing around with your accomplice will give you a lot of minutes to chuckle and test your cutthroat soul. Games can be hot, as well. Think strip poker or Twister. No difference either way. Game on!

Stare at the television and Motion pictures

Staring at the television and motion pictures together is perhaps of the least difficult action you can do following some serious time work. In any case, be certain it's simply you two, sitting together and clasping hands. No contraptions. No announcements or Instagram posts.

It's an incredible chance to cuddle and draw nearer while accomplishing something as straightforward as watching a Netflix series or film.

Attempt a Couples Back rub

Turn on some loosening up music, faint the lights, and alternate giving each other a back rub. To focus on a full-body knead, you can attempt a hand or foot back rub, and see where it takes you.

The exercises you partake in together needn't bother with to be a great deal of work. Simply hanging out unwinding, perusing, or staring at the TV can be charming.

Center around Your Relationship

Doing things together that are explicitly fixated on your relationship can likewise be an extraordinary method for working on your bond. A few thoughts you should investigate:

Go for a Stroll Through A world of fond memories

You've spent a great deal of years together and there are something else to come. Set aside some margin to audit your coexistence. Look at your PDA camera roll, Facebook photographs, or Instagram shots, and investigate your most memorable pictures together.

Think back pretty much everything you've done and puts you've been together throughout the long term, and continue to glance through until you arrive at your latest photographs all together.

Reestablish Your Commitments

Searching for something to do together that is somewhat more intricate? Reestablish your promises before loved ones or have a confidential function in your parlor. Restoring your commitments is an extraordinary sign of the security you have with one another, In the event that you have children, it's a pleasant method for integrating them into your function, particularly assuming they missed it the initial time around!

Visit Your Accomplice's Old neighborhood

Going to your accomplice's old neighborhood is an extraordinary method for diving more deeply into their young life. Regardless of whether you feel like you definitely have a deep understanding of your accomplice, seeing them in their old neighborhood setting will assist you with interfacing more profound. Trade humiliating youth stories or significant family recollections as you investigate old home bases together.

Investigating recollections together, reestablishing your responsibility, and visiting places that are extraordinary and developmental to your accomplice are only a couple of ways of hanging out and reinforce your relationship simultaneously.

Consistently is a festival of your relationship. Commend those minutes. Write in your schedule to commend your most memorable date, the date you got ready for marriage and, obviously, your wedding. Yet in addition make certain to celebrate other life minutes. In the event that your accomplice gets an advancement, cook an extraordinary dinner to celebrate. In the event that you finish your yearly test with no problem at all, partake in a night out together.

We frequently hide these normal life minutes away from plain view, yet praising them as they happen is one more method for commending you, your companion, your family, and the existence you have together.

CHAPTER 7

Part ways.

You take an earthenware course while your companion plays hockey; you play span and your accomplice gathers stamps. You don't need to adore all that your accomplice loves, however you in all actuality do need to permit him/her the opportunity to seek after treasured leisure activities. A special reward is that different interests can create interest between you. The vast majority in close connections like doing things together consistently. However, some of the time having time separated in a relationship is sound.

time separated in a relationship

The general purpose of a relationship is to be together, correct? You need to see one another, go on dates, travel, and so forth. In any case, sometimes, time separated in a relationship is crucial. Getting to know each other can make a ton of strain, particularly in a heartfelt connection.

What really does time separated in a relationship mean?

By separation, we don't mean you ought to attempt to have a far-removed relationship or not talk for quite a long time at a time. Time separated in a relationship will be different for everybody. As far as some might be concerned, that might mean having a young ladies' or alternately folks' night out one time per week. It could mean making "personal time." For other people, it very well may be going out traveling with your companions for the end of the week.

Investing all of your free energy with your accomplice can come down on your relationship. It might in fact make you lose your freedom if you don't watch out. [Read: 20 solid assumptions in a relationship that guarantee you have a decent love life]

The most effective method to be aware in the event that you really want time separated in a relationship

The general purpose of being seeing someone so you're in good company on the planet, correct? You generally have your individual to have some good times and appreciate existence with. Thus, you probably won't actually understand that you want time separated on the grounds that it is illogical to the very reason we have close connections. However, being together every minute of every day isn't really solid. It tends to be, yet provided that the two accomplices truly partake in getting to know one another. Nonetheless, most couples need some time alone to do whatever they might want to do some of the time.

Thus, you could not deliberately realize that you ought to part ways from your better half. Here are a few signs to search for to check whether you want a bit of personal time.

You get irritated with your accomplice without any problem

At the point when we initially begin dating somebody, we own them "rose-shaded glasses." as such, we just see their great characteristics and not their terrible ones. That doesn't mean they don't have them, yet we either disregard them or simply don't see it. Thus, assuming you end up getting irritated with a great deal of things your accomplice does out of nowhere, this is an indication that you really want some separation. In the event that each time they leave their socks on the floor or make a sound as if to speak resembles nails on a blackboard, then you truly need to want to invest some energy all alone for some time. [Read: Does he really want space? The unobtrusive signs folks give when they need space]

You pine for alone time

At the point when you are with your accomplice constantly, you persuade no chance to be without anyone else. Perhaps you need to observe all the Network programs and films they need to watch, and none of your own. Or then again, best case scenario, you need to think twice about. In any case, assuming you're fantasizing about what it might be want to have the house or television all to yourself, regardless of whether for a couple of hours, then that is one of the signs you want time separated in a relationship.

You miss your companions

It is normal to not consider our companions to be a lot of in another close connection. We're so enamored and made up for lost time in our new accomplice that we can't get enough of them. What's more, subsequently, spending time with our companions kind of goes by the wayside. In any case, assuming your companions are calling attention to that they never see you any longer, and you concur, then now is the ideal time to reserve some margin for yourself. It's beneficial to have a healthy lifestyle, and that incorporates various individuals as well, in addition to your accomplice. [Read: When a young lady says she wants space - What she means and what she anticipates from her guy]

You feel covered

In the event that you feel like you can do nothing without your accomplice close by, then, at that point, you presumably are feeling covered. On the off chance that you couldn't go to the supermarket without them needing to go with you, then this is simply excessively. You would rather not feel like you have an awesome time and chain appended to your leg.

You hate your accomplice however much you used to

Everybody has a special first night ease in their heartfelt connection. Thus, it's typical for it to wear off sooner or later. It could keep going up to several years, or it could wear off in two or three months. However, in any case, it will wear off at last. However, assuming you're in the period after the vacation stage has finished and you are loathing them as much any longer, then that is bad. You ought to in any case need to associate with them. In the event that you're not feeling as such, then, at that point, now is the right time to get some time separated in your relationship.

How long separated is sound seeing someone?

This is a troublesome inquiry to respond to, for the most part since all couples are unique. For instance, a few couples get to know each other, yet the two of them appreciate it that way. And afterward a few couples part ways, and they prefer it as such. Then, at that point, there are the ones who have to a greater degree a fair organization, with equivalent time together and separated. Thus, the more significant thing to contemplate is the degree of bliss for both of you. To be day in and day out and the other one necessities a great deal of room, then that won't function admirably. In any case, if the two individuals have any desire to be together day in and day out or potentially like a ton of alone time, then, at that point, that would function admirably. It truly relies upon whether both of your requirements are being satisfied. In the event that they are, change nothing. In any case, on the off chance that they're not, then you presumably need to have a serious talk and arrange how long separated you want in the relationship. [Read: How to give space in a relationship without floating separated.

As may be obvious, there truly is no such thing as the "awesome" measure of time spent together or separated. It very relies upon on the off chance that you two can agree for what works for both of you as a team.

What occurs on the off chance that you don't part ways in a relationship?

Have you at any point gone on an excursion with a companion and toward its finish, you are tired of them? They might not misunderstand done everything except a portion of their propensities simply begin to make you insane. To such an extent that you would rather not converse with them for seven days a while later! This can happen when you invest a ton of constant energy with somebody. Rather than valuing one another and anticipating hanging out, you get irritated by seemingly insignificant details like their steady channel flipping or knuckle breaking. On the off chance that you don't require even a couple of hours seven days from your accomplice, these little disturbances that truly shouldn't influence your relationship can hinder the bliss you would have in any case.

why you really want time separated in a relationship

Without healthy separation, all of your life is relying upon your relationship. And on second thought of partaking in your time together, you become exhausted or chafed. However, on the off chance that you actually aren't persuaded, investigate a portion of these justifications for why you really want time separated in a relationship.

You want to miss one another

This might sound senseless, yet missing each other even only for one day can offer a great deal to your relationship. You might have gotten so used to being around your accomplice that you've begun underestimating them. Time separated in a relationship can reignite that energy of needing to be together as opposed to having it be natural.

You can anticipate your time together

Hoping to invest all your free energy with your accomplice makes generally your time together unsurprising. In any case, when you have separation, you can anticipate your next night out. Expecting seeing your accomplice, yet in addition accomplishing something fun together keeps things fascinating and keeps a trench from shaping.

You take advantage of each and every second

Couples that are significant distance take advantage of each and every second together in light of the fact that they realize it won't keep going long. Furthermore, assuming you take additional time separated in a relationship, you will start to do that as well. Indeed, it is good to be with your accomplice while you are simply relaxing near or going shopping for food. Be that as it may, after a brief period separated, you connect more with one another. Sitting together staring at the television and looking at your telephone isn't taking advantage of your together time.

You can zero in on yourself

Long haul connections can make each accomplice lose some of their personality. You become so reliant upon your accomplice and your relationship that you fail to remember who you are all alone. You might try and begin to feel awkward going out without help from anyone else, or in any event, getting things done all alone, in light of the fact that you're so used to having your accomplice around. Yet, when you set aside some margin to zero in on your leisure activities and yourself, you offer more to the relationship. Assuming you lose yourself in your relationship and it closes, you self-destruct. You want a piece of yourself to exist beyond the relationship. Time separated keeps up with that freedom. [Read: Am I mutually dependent? 14 signs you're tenacious and violating boundaries]

You can zero in on your kinships

You presumably have that companion that ditches you at whatever point they are seeing someone. They drop plans, they go quiet in the gathering visit, and you don't hear from them except if their soul mate is away.

could do without it when others do this, so don't do this without anyone's help. Contingent upon your accomplice to satisfy your life comes down on them and the relationship. Having your companions to depend on and vent to or simply unwind with is indispensable for a sound relationship.

You won't require an excruciating break

We realize that pondering a potential separation sucks. Yet, on the off chance that you have made your accomplice your entire life, the separation is multiple times more awful. Without time separated in a relationship, separating is so terrible on the grounds that you are rearranging as long as you can remember without help from anyone else with no other notable individual in your life. Along these lines, in addition to the fact that time is separated helpful assuming things go south, however it

CHAPTER 8

Be companions with your accomplice.

The way to conjugal joy and achievement is companionship. Probably the main parts of this kind of companionship are knowing one another personally, exhibiting love and regard for one another consistently, and really appreciating each other's conversation.

Being a dearest companion implies keeping an eye out for what is best for them. It implies supporting them through various challenges. It is appreciating each other's conversation, making each other chuckle, and working and playing great together. Building a companionship with your life partner is crucial for an enduring marriage.

"Companionship is a type of closeness. It addresses a sharing, a transparency, an eagerness to be helpless. It requires a level of trust. Companions show minding to each other by their accessibility, their care."

KEYS TO Construct A Companionship WITH YOUR Life partner

Hang out. Lay out a period every week, then monitor it with your lives! Alright, perhaps not with your lives. You get the point, it's significant. Try not to permit it "adaptable" to different obligations or occasions that surface.

Investigate each other's advantages. Purposefully concentrate on the things that impact your better half or spouse and energetically go along with them. It might take some penance on your part, particularly in the event that it's not your favorite, but rather the outcomes are totally worth the effort.

Phenomenal correspondence is a vital aspect for building a kinship with your companion. Relationships that share really about issues, whether positive or testing, fabricate more grounded connections.

Recognize and confirm characteristics that you love about one another. Try not to expect they definitely know. Keep in touch with them a note, text, or face to face.

Play together! Giggling and fun are keys to building a companionship with your life partner.

Commend each other's disparities. Shock! You're not duplicates. Acknowledge and permit each other to act naturally without judgment.

Support one another. Help each other succeed. Expect traps. Likewise, bump or boot each other along.

Trust, responsibility and common regard ought to be really important in the space of connections, sex, and funds.

Be delicate with one another. Being closest companions with your life partner implies feeding and really focusing on each other. It gives solace. Building a companionship with your mate makes it conceivable to identify, relate, lift each other up in troublesome times.

Be straightforward with each other. Try not to restrict your discussions to revealing the occasions of the day. Be genuine with how you feel.

Cooperate on projects. In addition to the fact that you hanging out, however you are likewise fabricating group abilities.

Figure out how to battle fair. Being closest companions with your mate doesn't mean you won't ever contend. Conflicts in marriage can be a structure block to a more grounded relationship in the event that you figure out how to battle fair in marriage. Use clashes to hone and clean your companionship.

Lay out day to day propensities, particularly asking together.

Shared interests and values are a vital aspect for building a kinship with your companion.

Advance together and from each other.

CHAPTER 9

The Nicknames.

Roses, candy, cards, and gifts are awesome badge of adoration, however assuming that you truly believe your sentiment should endure, you should rehearse some marriage-saving advances. Wesley Walker instructs couples to make use concerning charm terms.

A charm is a cherishing or friendly word or expression that you share with somebody you love.

Pet names are awesome comments. Darlings use them to communicate their profound private affections for one another. Furthermore, they just do it after they have been together for some time. Families and old buddies use them in light of the fact that once more, they express friendship and it is generally in a relaxed environment. Nicknames are utilized to reassure individuals and be a type of endorsement, sympathy, and to show interest.

Individuals use pet names for various reasons, large numbers of which are expected to accomplish a shared objective: reinforcing the obligations of a relationship. These connections can be non-romantic (e.g., between old buddies), familial (e.g., between kin), or heartfelt (e.g., between a couple). Utilizing these terms infers a nearby, warm connection between the gatherings, and they can act as a low-stress method for showing your love for somebody.

Lovebug, Darling, Darling, Honey are a few sweet expressions of charm

CHAPTER 10

Say "I love you" consistently.

This is particularly significant when you're not feeling the vibe of adoration; at these times, you need to produce it effectively. Saying those three little words, and performing adoring motions, will warm both your and your life partner's hearts. It's just suitable that we tell our friends and family simply that we love them. However, not we all are accustomed to saying those three little words.

Love is inferred, you could say. However, there's valid justification to say it, as well. "It's the oxygen for the relationship,". "Telling someone you love them takes care of the relationship, keeps it alive."

It supports your sentiments and reminds your friends and family - whether your life partner, darling, kid or parent - that you are there for themselves and that they make a difference to you. "What individuals are truly searching for is close to home presence," . We can genuinely be standing right close to somebody but be miles separated inwardly.

People are made for association, "We are continually moving in the direction of or away from one another in connections."

Significance of saying I love you

Why say I love you? For what reason does saying "I Love You" matter? What's the significance of talking about 'I love you'? What difference does it make that we require investment to let our companions know that we love them? It's not difficult to fall into this psychological example. We're with them, correct? Is it true that we are as yet hitched? We get things done for them, get them gifts, and invest energy with them. Shouldn't they just, indeed, realize that we love them? Regardless of whether you believe that they know, saying it makes a difference. At the point when you let your companion know that you love them, you reaffirm your affection for them, yet in addition for your relationship. You let them know that you esteem their presence and your marriage. It's tied in with underlining care, responsibility, and appreciation.

There's a significance of saying 'I love you' in light of the fact that not saying "I love you" can make distance among you and start dissolving the association that you feel with each other. You might start to feel undervalued or that your life partner doesn't esteem the relationship. Fortunately changing the worldview is straightforward.

How would you say I love you?

1. Be careful and say it

In the wake of understanding the significance of saying I love you, maybe the absolute most significant hint is this - be aware of the times that you don't say "I love you" and focus on evolving it. Basically trying to say those three little words all the more frequently can significantly affect your relationship and what you receive in return. Take time consistently to let your life partner know that you love them, yet don't do it in passing. Be purposeful. Make it significant.

For example, put your hand on their shoulder, investigate their eyes, and purposely say, "I love you." Hold eye to eye connection while you're saying it and a short time later.

How frequently would it be advisable for you to say it?

There's actually no firmly established reply. There's no need to focus on keeping track of who's winning or arriving at some fanciful day to day limit where saying those words mystically reinforces your relationship. It's tied in with making a careful association with your mate through those three words and the feeling behind them.

www.ingramcontent.com/pod-product-compliance
Lightning Source LLC
LaVergne TN
LVHW050346160826
845677LV00014B/3826

* 9 7 9 8 3 6 9 6 4 3 0 9 9 *